THE SQUATTERS —By "PLUM"

Pompey were at this time fourth from bottom of Division One.

On 30th November 1946, Pompey defeated Charlton Athletic 3-0 at Fratton Park.

Pompey had been floundering near the bottom of Division One but results were beginning to improve.

Pompey made a good start to 1947, winning 2-0 at home to Bolton Wanderers.

At Christmas, the threat of relegation was hovering over Fratton Park but 1947 had seen Pompey make a steady rise up the First Division table.

On 15th March, Liverpool came to Fratton Park and recorded a 2-1 victory. This was Pompey's first league defeat in eight matches.

This cartoon shows how Pompey climbed the First Division ladder in 1947. Remember "The Squatter" was told to move on in November 1946 (No. 1).

Bob Jackson took over as Pompey manager in the summer of 1947. He led the Club to two successive League Championships in 1949 and 1950, leaving Fratton Park in 1952 to manage Hull City.

New signing Ike Clarke scored after only six minutes of his Pompey debut in the previous week's clash with Aston Villa at Fratton Park.

Plum looks ahead to Pompey's visit to The Valley, where sure to be in goal for Charlton was Sam Bartram. The result was 2-2.

.. And They Said "Nothing Could Stop Arsenal!"

Heavy snow caused Pompey's home match with reigning League Champions Arsenal to be postponed. The re-arranged fixture was played in April and finished 0-0.

This was the opening day of the 1948-49 season - Pompey's Golden
Jubilee. What a season it proved to be.

Pompey Chairman Vernon Stokes had issued a message to the players, "Win the Championship for the Jubilee." They started the season with a 2-2 draw at Preston and followed it with a 4-0 home victory over Everton.

A 1-0 victory at Stoke the previous week put Pompey top of Division One for the first time since 1932.

Just proving that Pompey were not downhearted after their first defeat of the season.

At this time, Derby County were leading the First Division with Pompey in second place.

This was the day of Pompey's famous Jubilee match with Arsenal. Fratton Park was inundated with messages of congratulations.

Pompey's 4-1 victory over reigning League Champions Arsenal on 27th November 1948 was one of the most memorable in the Club's history.

NEXT WEEK'S SOMETHING FOR THE 'TABLE'!

Pompey beat Preston North End 3-1 at Fratton Park on 18th December.

Pompey hit seven goals for the first time since the war when they beat Stockport County 7-0 in the FA Cup third round at Fratton Park.

Ike Clarke was Pompey's two-goal hero in the 2-1 FA Cup sixth round win over Derby County. The match was watched by a record Fratton Park crowd of 51,385.

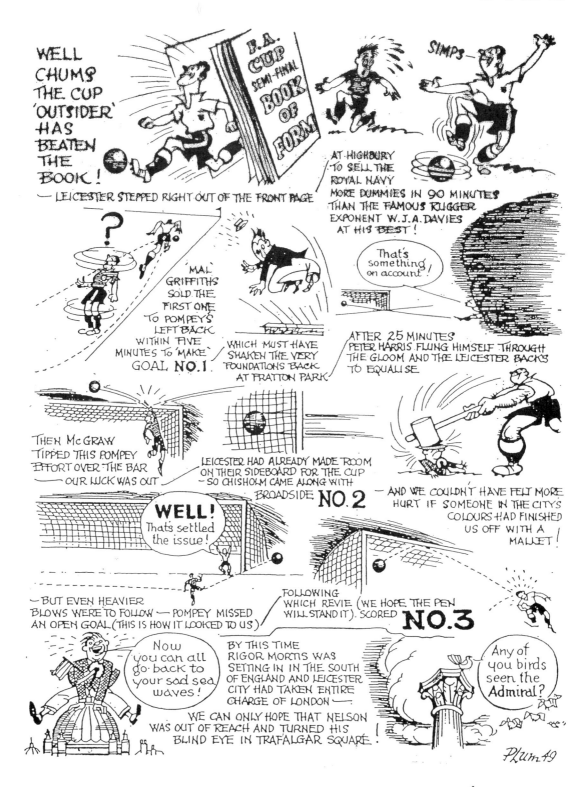

Pompey went close to becoming the first club of the 20th century to win the League and Cup Double. But they were beaten 3-1 by Second Division strugglers Leicester City in the FA Cup Semi-Final at Highbury. The result goes down as one of the most disappointing in the Club's history.

Pompey put the Cup disappointment behind them and looked forward to Easter home matches with Birmingham City and Wolves. They won them both.

Pompey were now almost home and dry as Football League Champions.

A 2-1 victory at Bolton the previous Saturday clinched the first of two successive Football League titles.

On 30th April, with Pompey having already made sure of winning the League Championship, Club President Field Marshall Montgomery was presented with the Football League Championship trophy at Fratton Park. Pompey won their home match with Huddersfield Town 2-0.

. . . THE ONE THAT GOT AWAY
— WITH A POINT

After recording a 3-1 win at Newcastle on the opening day of the season, it was a disappointment for Pompey to only scramble a 1-1 draw at home to Manchester City.

Pompey had never beaten Birmingham City at St. Andrews until 8th October 1949 when they won 3-0.

Plum was looking ahead to the visit to Chelsea on 5th November.

It had been another good week for Pompey. They crushed Chelsea 4-1 at Stamford Bridge and Jack Froggatt had been selected to play for England for the first time.

On 28th January 1950, Pompey beat Grimsby Town 5-0 at Fratton Park in the FA Cup fourth round. This was Cliff Parker's match. Drafted into the side only because Peter Harris was unfit, the match showed that there was plenty of football left in the veteran.

Plum describes Pompey's 2-1 victory over Liverpool at Fratton Park on 22nd April 1950.

Pompey's 5-1 win over Aston Villa at Fratton Park on this day meant they finished above Wolverhampton Wanderers on goal average, thus retaining the League Championship trophy.

The Right Prescription!   —By 'Plum'

Pompey's early season form was hardly worthy of League Champions but on 16th September 1950 they turned on the style to beat Stoke City 5-1 at Fratton Park.

Four-tune Favours Wolves! —By Plum

The 4-1 defeat by Wolves on 28th October 1950 was Pompey's first of the season at Fratton Park and only their third since Boxing Day 1947.

Championship Reflection!   —By Plum

Before the day's 3-3 home draw with Charlton Athletic, Pompey were lying fourteenth in the First Division table.

A mighty roar from the 49,000 fans greeted Duggie Reid's goal against Tottenham Hotspur seven minutes after the start of the Easter Monday fixture. The final score was 1-1.

Plum pays tribute to Jack Froggatt after the Yorkshireman had been selected to play for England at centre-half.

On the day of the Grand National - 7th April 1951 - Pompey drew 0-0 with Sunderland at Fratton Park.

" . . . old timer from the North Stand. His lordship says having had to cough up for one of those new fangled season tickets . . . he's not going to have his blinking seat pinched! "

In 1951, Pompey introduced season-tickets for all league matches at Fratton Park.

A late Marcel Gaillard goal won the match against Charlton Athletic on 25th August 1951.

Wolves were the next week's visitors to Fratton Park. They defeated Pompey 3-2.

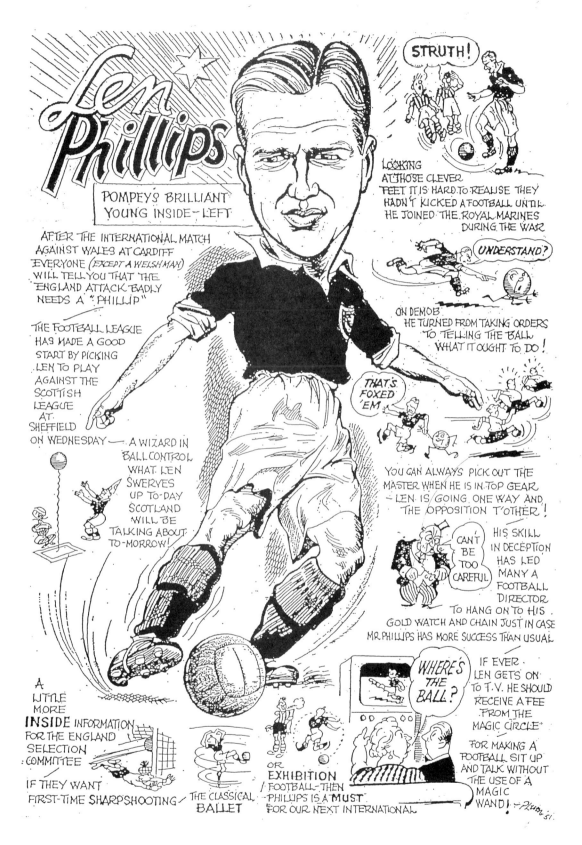

Plum pays tribute to Len Phillips, arguably the most gifted player in Pompey history.

Matches were now being broadcast to hospitals from Fratton Park. The match between Pompey and Aston Villa on 29th September 1951 was the first football match ever to be broadcast on Hospital Radio.

On 8th December 1951, Pompey drew 2-2 at home to Burnley.

The Boxing Day clash between Pompey and Arsenal finished 1-1.

Perhaps it's only a rumour that Manager Bob Jackson is bringing out his famous collection of lucky bow-ties to play for Pompey in the F.A. Cup-tie at Fratton Park next Saturday.

Just as former Pompey manager Jack Tinn was famous for his lucky spats, Bob Jackson was well known for wearing bow-ties. Pompey won the match with Lincoln City 4-0.

This was FA Cup fourth round day. Pompey beat Notts County 3-1 at Meadow Lane.

"Keep pegging away, Pompey . . . . 'ope it keeps fine for you!"

When this cartoon featured in the Football Mail, Pompey were in fourth place, five points behind Manchester United. Both teams ended the season in the same positions.

Pompey's entire half-back line of Jimmy Scoular, Jack Froggatt and Jimmy Dickinson all played in the Scotland v England match at Hampden Park on this day. England won 2-1.

" . . . the cap fits beautifully, the right man in the right colours . . .
only wants a cup in each hand to complete the picture!"

Eddie Lever was appointed manager of Pompey in 1952. He held the position for six years.

" Sorry Sir! . . . Someone shouted taxi and they were off! There's no holding these boys since Pompey beat Bolton Wanderers 5—0!"

On the previous Saturday, Pompey recorded a 5-0 victory at Bolton.

On 11th October 1952, Pompey beat Manchester City 2-1.

Pompey were knocked out of the FA Cup by Burnley and so failed to emulate their 1939 triumph. We're still waiting.

The previous week, Pompey beat Sheffield United 6-2 at Fratton Park with Peter Harris scoring four of the goals and the other two coming from Johnny Gordon.

Pat Neil was still a schoolboy when he was playing on the left-wing for Pompey's First Division side.

Plum pays tribute to three Pompey players and Club Director Syd Leverett, who was a member of the Board from 1912 until his death in 1959.

On 12th November 1956, England winger Tom Finney produced a devastating display to help Preston North End to a 2-0 victory over Pompey at Fratton Park.

THE MYSTERIOUS UNFATHOMABLE

GORDON DALE

THE MAGICIAN WHO IS A NOVEMBER HANDICAP TO THE BEST DEFENCES!

THE ONLY FOOTBALLER WHO CAN FOOL THE MAESTRO STANLEY MATTHEWS AT HIS OWN GAME!

THE MAN'S UNCANNY

POINTS

A SHORT STROLL. A MAGIC PASS — AND HEY PRESTO! IT'S A GOAL! LET'S HOPE HE'S GOT PLENTY LEFT UP HIS SLEEVE — POMPEY NEED ALL HIS TRICKS.

Outside-left Gordon Dale was one of the most skilful players to ever play for Pompey. Dale had recently played a match at centre-forward, hence the number nine.

NO MATCH ON CHRISTMAS DAY!
HAVE A GOOD TIME POMPEY — YOU DESERVE IT!

The match at Luton on Boxing Day was postponed. When the fixture took place in March, the Hatters won 1-0.

On Easter Monday 1957, Pompey travelled to Cardiff and won 2-0 to complete a 100% record from their three holiday fixtures. Winning those six points meant that relegation to the Second Division was avoided.

Pompey were drawn at home to Aldershot in the FA Cup third round. They won the match 5-1.

On 18th January 1958, relegation threatened Pompey earned a precious victory over Manchester City thanks to two goals from Ray Crawford.

During his spell as Pompey manager, Freddie Cox was heavily criticized for tactical plans that failed to bring results, but occasionally things came right on the field as they did when Leicester City were beaten 4-1.

Already doomed to relegation from the First Division, winning the FA Cup and two successive League Championships seemed a very long time ago.

On this day, Pompey were staring the Third Division in the face as they entertained Hull City at Fratton Park. The match ended 1-1 and relegation was eventually avoided.

Caretaker-manager Bill Thompson made two inspired signings in the shape of Allan Brown and Johnny Gordon. The pair arrived too late for Pompey to stave off relegation to the Third Division, but the contribution they made in helping the side return as champions at the first attempt can never be over-estimated.

NEW BOYS AT FRATTON PARK WHO WILL HELP BLAZE THE TRAIL TO THE SECOND DIVISION

DAVE DODSON OUTSIDE-LEFT FROM SWANSEA

DAVE PLAYED FOR ARSENAL, AND PARTNERED JIMMY GREAVES IN THE ENGLAND YOUTH TEAM!

SCORED WITHIN 20 SECONDS - THE FIRST TIME HE TOUCHED THE BALL FOR POMPEY

TONY BARTON OUTSIDE-RIGHT SIGNED FROM NOTTS. FOREST

WATCH THESE YOUNG GO-GETTERS IN THE NEW POMPEY LINE-UP. ALL SET TO KEEP THEIR POSITION 'ON' TOP'

ROY SMITH FROM HEREFORD UNITED

"DICK BARTON ALWAYS FINDS HIS MAN. MADE THE PASS FOR DODSON TO OPEN HIS ACCOUNT

ROY SIGNED FOR POMPEY ON WEDNESDAY. HAD A BIG REPUTATION AS AN INSIDE-LEFT IN THE SOUTHERN LEAGUE, PLAYED FOR WEST HAM.

Here, Plum introduces three newly-signed players. David Dodson scored 21 goals in 62 games for Pompey and Tony Barton netted 36 goals in 144 appearances before a knee injury, sustained in 1966 ended his career. Roy Smith suffered two broken legs and was forced to retire after making only eleven appearances in which he scored five goals.

Keith Blackburn made 37 league and cup appearances, scoring 8 goals in a four year spell at Fratton Park.

Ron Saunders was a prolific goalscorer during his six years with Pompey, scoring 156 goals in 258 appearances. In October 1963 he hit hat-tricks in two successive matches – a 5-2 home win over Newcastle United and a 6-3 victory away to Leyton Orient.

ANOTHER RISING STAR
RAY HIRON

POMPEY'S NEW RAY OF HOPE
20 YEARS YOUNG
6 FEET 1 INCH OF
FOOTBALL AMBITION

IN LESS THAN 2 YEARS

~ GRADUATED FROM THE
GOSPORT LEAGUE - HAMPSHIRE
LEAGUE - POMPEY RESERVES
~ TO THE POMPEY FIRST TEAM

SCORED 39 GOALS FOR
FAREHAM TOWN
LAST SEASON

TODAY'S
BIG
QUESTION
MARK

CAN RAY TAKE OVER THE
MANTLE OF RON SAUNDERS
TOP SCORER FOR POMPEY
· NOW TRANSFERRED
TO WATFORD ?

"HEAVEN'S LIGHT OUR
GUIDE" IS THE
CITY'S MOTTO

RAISE US RAY

"HIRON'S
HAT TRICKS"
MAY WELL
BE POMPEY'S
SALVATION !

RAY CAN BECOME THE
GUIDING STAR IN THE BID
FOR THE FIRST DIVISION

Ray Hiron joined Pompey from Fareham Town in 1964. He made 383 league and cup appearances and scored 119 goals before moving to Reading on a free transfer in 1975.

With five matches of the season remaining, Pompey were desperately fighting to avoid the drop into the Third Division.

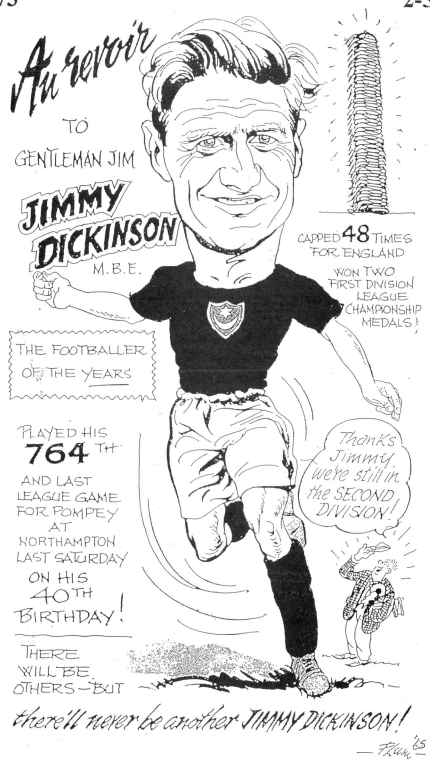

On 24th April 1965, Jimmy Dickinson's magnificent playing career came to a close. Never sent off, booked or even spoken to by a referee, Dickinson was awarded the M.B.E. in 1964 for his services to the game. His last match took place at Northampton on his 40th birthday and a 1-1 draw saved Pompey from relegation to the Third Division.

HARRY HARRIS

THE NEW POMPEY CAPTAIN

MAN WITH A MISSION

TO SCALE THE HEIGHTS OF THE SECOND DIVISION

Lead on Harry and GOOD LUCK TO THE ELITE!

Harry Harris took over the Club captaincy from Jimmy Dickinson and this day was the first of the 1965-66 season. The team gave him a grand start as skipper by beating Plymouth Argyle 4-1 at Fratton Park.

Declining attendances at Fratton Park were becoming a source of worry for the Club's Board of Directors.

For the umpteenth time, Pompey were bracing themselves for an end of season relegation battle.

Southampton were promoted to the First Division in 1966 while Pompey were still attempting to make a return to the top-flight since being relegated in 1959.

Johnny
GORDON

PLAYED IN HIS
400TH
LEAGUE MATCH FOR
POMPEY LAST NIGHT!

A 100 PER CENTER
IN THE "DICKINSON
MOULD"

HAPPY TO PLAY
ANYWHERE IN
THE TEAM!

... AND
JOHNNY
GOES
MARCHING
ON!

Johnny Gordon made his 400th league appearance for Pompey in the previous evening's 4-1 victory over Middlesbrough at Fratton Park. Gordon retired in 1967 after scoring 116 goals in 486 outings for the Club.

Having won one and lost three of their first four home matches, it was hoped that Pompey could give the fans something to celebrate the following Saturday when they entertained Millwall. Unfortunately, the Lions went away with a 1-0 victory.

Having abandoned the youth policy and finding it difficult to find cash for transfer fees, the Club hoped to strengthen the squad by the way of player-exchange deals.

Despite Pompey going down 3-1 at Wolverhampton, the fans who
had travelled to Molineux gave their team encouragement for the
entire ninety minutes of the game.

Pompey's season had not started too well so a home victory over Ipswich Town came as a relief. It began a run of five unbeaten games.

Financial worries were never far away from Fratton Park.

Having won three and drawn two of the previous five matches, there was hope at Fratton Park that Pompey could push for a promotion place.

In the match at Fratton Park the following Saturday, Norwich City were certainly surprised for, after leading 3-0 and cruising, Pompey hit back to draw 3-3. Plymouth Argyle were beaten 2-1 by Pompey at Fratton on Boxing Day.

In January 1967, Pompey paid a Club record £25,000 for Nick Jennings from Plymouth Argyle. The outside-left made 227 appearances and scored 50 goals before joining Exeter City in 1974.

George Smith's dream of turning Pompey into a First Division outfit in five years failed to materialise. He left the Club in 1971 and top-flight football did not return to Fratton Park until 1987.

In 1967, Pompey abandoned their famous blue and white for **an all blue strip with red and white trimmings**. The change seemed to bring the team better results with three points gained from the season's first two matches and the 1967-68 campaign was the Club's most exciting for many years.

At this time, Pompey were riding high in the Second Division while Saints were struggling in Division One.

In 1968, Fratton Park offered a creche so that children could be taken care of while the parents were watching the match.

For the first time since losing their First Division status in 1959, Pompey had a genuine hope of achieving promotion back to the top-flight. But from those thirteen remaining matches, they could only achieve three wins and four draws, eventually finishing in fifth place.

Pompey manager George Smith missed the 1-0 FA Cup victory over Fulham because of 'flu. There was no Sky TV, Ceefax or even Local Radio in those days so Mr. Smith would have needed to rely on the telephone for up-to-date news.

THE BIG SQUEEZE   By Plum

Crowds at Fratton Park were higher than they had been for years with 44,050 having attended the FA Cup fourth round tie against Fulham and another 40,000 plus gate promised for the following week's fifth round clash with West Bromwich Albion.

On this day, a crowd of over 42,000 watched Pompey go down 2-1 to West Bromwich Albion in the FA Cup fifth round.

On 30th November 1968, Pompey produced a brilliant display to beat Millwall 3-0 at Fratton Park, knocking the Lions off the top of the Second Division.

SAFEST PAIR OF HANDS
OUTSIDE THE BANK OF ENGLAND

John Milkins

POMPEY'S LAST LINE
OF DEFENCE. MADE HIS
200TH LEAGUE AND
F.A. CUP APPEARANCE

TODAY!

AMBITION – TO PLAY
FOR POMPEY IN THE
FIRST DIVISION!

Plum '69

John Milkins made his Pompey debut as a 16 year-old and played in
389 competitive matches for the Club before being transferred to
Oxford United in 1974.   Unfortunately, he didn't achieve his
ambition of playing in the First Division.

Constantly suffering from financial worries, Portsmouth Football Club were always hoping a wealthy benefactor would arrive at Fratton Park.

Mike Trebilcock was dropped soon after scoring a hat-trick against Watford but on his return to face Blackburn Rovers later in the month, he grabbed three goals in eight minutes.

Pompey scrapped their youth and reserve sides in 1965 but at this time, the Club were planning to re-construct the youth and reserve set-up.

By 1971, hooliganism had sadly become part of football but at least 'Plum' could find a humorous side to the problem.